The Way Of Questions

Jack Ricchiuto

~ DesigningLife Books ~

Books by Jack Ricchiuto

Collaborative Creativity / 1996
Accidental Conversations / 2002
Project Zen / 2003
Appreciative Leadership / 2005
Mountain Paths / 2007
Conscious Becoming / 2008
Instructions From The Cook / 2009
The Stories That Connect Us / 2010
The Enchantment Of Casual Origins / 2011
The Joy Of Thriving / 2012
Ordinary Eyes / 2012
The Agile Canvas Field Guide / 2012
Abundant Possibilities / 2013
The Power Of Circles / 2013
Making Sense Of Time / 2014
Beyond Recipes / 2014
Focus / 2015
Smarter Together / 2015
Ideas / 2015
The Art Of Conversations / 2016
The Way Of Questions / 2017

3 | The Way Of Questions

The Way Of Questions

Published by DesigningLife Books

1020 Kenilworth Avenue

Cleveland OH 44113 USA

Copyright 2017 Jack Ricchiuto

ISBN 978-154132143-4

Paperback

1. Psychology. Curiosity. Change.

I. Title

First edition, January 15, 2017

Printed in the USA

Production: CreateSpace

Cover: Tia Andrako

Content

The nature of questions

The world of questions

always the beautiful answer
who asks a more beautiful question

e.e cummings

Invitation

There is much about this world our great-grandparents might not have imagined possible.

We have daily access to more news and updates than they had from a year's worth of newspapers and radio programming. Neighborhoods in any climate can become completely power and food self-sufficient. With smart phones, we can be seen and treated in real time by medical staff on the other side of the planet.

Our houses and pets can text us at work when they need some kind of attention. We can pull out of our back pockets a world of knowledge, music and film. Soon, an elderly family member who can no longer drive can text for a safer-than-humans driverless car whenever they need one. We can continue to be gifted by their freedom to be engaged.

It's unclear what's next. Uncertainty is the new certainty. We daily stumble on new puzzles that perplex us, new dilemmas that devil us and new crossroads that cross us. We are particularly baffled how with change as life's prime constant, we still have problems that persist despite even well-intended efforts otherwise.

Problems that most persist, personally and collectively, are those we keep trying to solve with the wrong questions. When we struggle for new perspectives, it's when we use the wrong questions to navigate new uncertainties. The wrong questions are the old questions.

Old questions don't have the power to unfold new insights or deeper understandings of anything. Only new questions have this power. Navigating new landscapes of uncertainty requires the new literacy of crafting new questions.

The Primacy of Questions

Our questions define us

No matter what our path so far, each of us has had moments we considered success. We successfully learned, endured or accomplished something.

When we succeed, it is because we get our questions right. The questions we lived in each instance of success guided us from uncertainty to what we wanted to see possible. We always do our best based on our questions at the time. The quality of our lives is equal to the quality of our questions.

One of the lessons of our successes is that moving forward toward the possibilities that matter most to us does not necessarily require being a different person or having a different world. It requires different questions.

I don't think it occurred to Thomas Edison of the light bulb, Tim Berners-Lee of the Internet or Steve Jobs of

Apple to change who they were or alter the world as it was before they dared to embark on world-changing journeys toward the possible impossible. What did occur to them was that no old questions were going to help them get to new perspectives that would revolutionize how we live, work, learn and connect.

The intention here is humble, however radical. It starts with a simple idea that if we want anything new in our life and world, we need new questions. Whatever we worry, whine or wish about, it will take new questions to achieve what will provoke our gratitude. Not even our most worn, old questions will carry us forward.

I've spend the last three decades working with people to make their work, communities and lives more vibrant. It is fascinating how in every context, as they navigated new levels of uncertainty, they achieved new levels of vibrancy when they moved from old to new questions. My work as writer helps them craft better questions that would lead to unpredictable breakthroughs.

I invite them to move from questions about deficiencies and grievances to questions about strengths and dreams. Losing faith in old questions that have no transformational power, new questions shift people from stuck to empowered.

Often beyond the horizons of commercial and social media headlines, there are people all over the world making wonderful differences.

They are the unsung people transforming neighborhoods, businesses, medicine, education, science, technology, consumer products, philanthropy, architecture, entrepreneurship and the arts. They are changing how we live, work, play, learn, design, interact, enjoy and see ourselves and the world.

They are not living lives of quiet acquiescence or the hope of helplessness. They dream unreasonable dreams beyond the small comforts of normal. What makes them different from the many around them who aren't? They're living from new questions.

As much as we romanticize about people who are inventive about their worlds and themselves, they don't necessarily have super powers, superior intellects or significant resource advantages. They have new questions. With respect for all the good that old questions have achieved so far, they understand that the old questions don't lead to new possibilities.

When we want to understand the secret to those we most admire for their unique contributions to the world, we simply consider the questions that shape them.

The old mythology was that our world is a reflection of our beliefs. It's a new perspective to consider that the state of our world and our lives isn't at root caused by our social, political and religious beliefs. Beliefs loom large because we talk more about them than we do our questions. Our beliefs are simply our best answers to our best questions.

Our questions intrinsically define us. When we want to change our lives, we change our questions.

Things are as they are because of our questions. Every history is a history of questions shaping beliefs shaping destinies. To sustain our questions is to sustain how things are. Changing things happens when we change our questions.

Learning our way into the future

In more certain times, we can predict and repeat our way into the future. Old beliefs and questions work. They are trusty guides to survival and success.

As it becomes more clear that uncertainty is life's constant, empowered by new questions, we learn our way into the future we want to see. The more uncertain our future, the more our survival and success depends on a passion for learning new perspectives.

This is a perspective supported by fascinating stories. Thomas Edison's most impactful breakthrough was designing the utility system that could power a city of light bulbs. Tim Berners-Lee's incubation of the internet changed how we live, work and learn in more ways than we can predict. Steve Jobs got us to reimagine how we could connect to the world's published knowledge as we curate and narrate our life.

Although they never met, they had much in common. They dedicated themselves to the kinds of new questions that catapulted them and their teams into a rare and fertile space of uncertainty. In this space, there are no predictive maps, formulas, experts or answers, only new questions.

They cast aside old questions for new ones. While people were trying to more vigorously answer old questions about how to engineer better candles, libraries and telephones, they were pursuing questions that had no precedent or popularity.

They ventured beyond old beliefs of what was possible. They learned their way into a new future. Someone had to learn how to empower whole new industries, scale global connectivity and place the breadth and depth of our digital footprints in the palms of our hands. They and their teams did just that.

Through new questions, they learned their way into these breakthroughs that would change the world. Their learning happened because they refused the seduction of old questions about power, connectivity and access in favor of new questions few others were living.

Their questions defined them and the world whose imaginations will never be the same. They learned how to navigate vast oceans of uncertainty to make the world as never before. They did it through countless iterations of new question-based learning.

Every new success we have enjoyed came about because we learned our way into it. Every time we help a friend, colleague or child arrive at a new ah-ha, it is because we help them realize a new question. Every time someone sparked a personal breakthrough insight for us, it was because they exposed us to a question we never before considered in that context.

New questions

We are daily amazed at the barrage of available information. Every day more than 4 million hours of content are uploaded to YouTube. Facebook hosts 4.3 billion messages. People do 6 billion Google searches and trade 200 billion emails. A day's worth of Tweets would fill a 10 million page book. We're just getting started.

We can spend whole lifetimes finding additional support for how right we are about what we already know and believe. In each case, if we spend time looking for and enjoying more evidence for our rightness, it's because we're living from old questions.

In new questions, we discover more about what we don't know. We can also spend whole lifetimes discovering a universe of what's beyond the horizon of what we already know and believe.

It's unknown how many of these represent answers to old questions, or how many raise new questions. Given the continuity in how people think and live, it's likely much of it represents answers to old questions. Much of this continuity derives from the social principle of belonging that we tend to live by the questions others we know live by.

Every innovator in every field of human endeavor stumbled on new answers from new questions. Every innovator in the arts, sciences, government, business, economics, entertainment, agriculture and medicine lived and live from new questions. They were more passionate about being curious for new perspectives than right in old perspectives.

If we want to be suspicious of anyone whose creativity we enjoy and admire, it's being suspicious that they're driven by questions few others are asking themselves.

There are a few classic ways to discover new questions. We can consider what we don't know. This includes what we know we don't know and what we think few if any people know. They can be things other people aren't curious about. We can turn any popular belief into any number of interesting new questions that accelerate us onto a new learning curve.

We can imagine what we think might be true and turn these possibilities into questions. This includes what we expect, assume and believe to be true. We can explore new areas of knowledge and exposure that spark new questions. This includes any kinds of browsing, scanning and traveling.

When I teach mindfulness, people discover that when they feel stuck about anything, they get unstuck just remembering that it's because at that time, they're living from the wrong questions, which are old questions.

As soon as they consider what they don't yet know, they feel more mindfully empowered. They move forward. The uncertainty of what they don't know becomes the magic to their flourishing as never before.

Not bad people

Why do we struggle as we do? Why do we still wrestle with the same questions parents and couples did millennials ago? Why would we feel like we never are or have enough? Why are we still a planet divided into haves and have-nots?

Why do we still have 2 billion people failing to thrive on less than US $2 a day while 62 people own as much wealth as the economic bottom half of people globally? Why do the vast majority of people worldwide work more hours with less passion, engagement and meaning in their work?

Why do we still have such barbaric violence destroying beautiful cities, cultures, families and lives? Why are more people in a crisis of faith relative to their governments and leaders?

We could argue that it would take an insane planet to pull this off. The question of whether people are basically good or bad is a very old question that, in the premise of this conversation, is likely to have little ability to lead to new perspectives.

If we argue anything, it could be that there are not good or bad people. There are only good and bad questions.

Good questions bring our the best in us. Bad questions bring out the worst in us. When we see people at their best, it's because they're operating from good questions. When we see people at their worst, it's because they're operating from bad questions. This single insight clears up a planet full of mystery about human motivation and behavior.

It just so happens that many of the bad questions are old questions. They might have made things better for some people in another time. They helped people navigate the uncertainty of that time. They don't help us navigate the uncertainty of this time.

Each of us struggles with uncertainty not because we lack goodness. We struggle because we're trying to navigate uncertainty with the wrong questions, the old questions. If we need anything, it's living instead from new questions.

Impatience

We live in an age of impatience. We crave instant conclusions. It's fast becoming a ubiquitous and invisible learning disability.

We like hearing or reading something and having the feeling that we have the whole story in a single sound bite. We delight in not needing to spend any further time understanding, knowing or learning anything else, anything beyond the surface of what's presented. We have little patience for anything deeper beyond the flash of our impatience. This is an age where efficiency is more important than beauty. Busyness is the new badge of honor.

The whole business about fake news is driving us crazy with the untenable possibility that we might have to become learning-abled beyond sound bites.

On the upside, conclusions seem to spare us from the throes of uncertainty. On the downside, instant answers keep us from new perspectives. No matter what the issue, if we're not learning something new, it's because we're living from old questions.

I can spend whole evenings in conclusion fests with any numbers of people on any variety of topics. I know people who can go for hours without tendering a new question of any kind. They curate cocktails of conclusions around the campfire of rightness. It helps if people look and sound more alike than not. This keeps uncertainty, and learning, off the table and outside the door.

If we don't have patience to create, much less give time to, new questions, we are destined to be constrained by old questions that have instant answers that already exist.

We're just beginning to realize that personal and global problems persist because of our naive faith in old questions and their easy answers that make deeper learning inconvenient at best and at worst threats to our most cherished assumptive beliefs.

One of the marrow differences between the character of old and new questions is that old questions seek further validation for beliefs we already live by. Theirs is a curiosity seeking new stories and facts proving what we already believe.

New questions seek new understanding for new perspectives. Their curiosity is about what we don't yet know by fact or belief. What else could we explore here? This is a simple, powerful question that moves us from old to new questions.

If we have a question we feel prepared to answer with no further reflection or research, it's likely an old question. If it's a question we feel unprepared for, it's likely a new question.

Humility

Humility is knowing what we don't know. It's that small pause after an instant conclusion where we allow ourselves to wonder what else might be true or possible.

Knowing what we don't know is a bit complex because beliefs and facts are things we know to be true, even though beliefs are assumptions requiring no facts. When we argue with people about their beliefs, we are arguing with what they trust to be true. For each of us on the planet, beliefs are as trustworthy as facts, and as certain.

Humility is interest in exploring the world beyond our facts or beliefs. It is curiosity about what we don't yet know. It is considering neither belief nor fact as definitive conclusions. It's an attitude of that's what we know so far. The more humility we live with, the more new questions we are capable of creating and discovering.

Humility doesn't make anything we know wrong. In humility we don't pretend to not know or believe what we honestly know and believe.

We simply allow ourselves to notice the universe of things we also don't actually know for sure. It's not denial; it's discovery.

It's the expectation that there might be more to know beyond what we already know. It's the provocative Zen suggestion that things are not as they appear, nor are they otherwise.

This is my 21st book. Each started with a degree of certainty about something, a rich broth of beliefs, stories and facts. As each book unfolded in reflection, research and conversations, new questions emerged and inspired new possibilities and more questions.

Making what I didn't know more important than what I did know was all it took to inspire and inform the path to new perspectives and new books.

Each published project concluded with new questions, many times leading to next projects. The more I knew in the end, the more clear I was on the more I didn't know. I continue to measure success in how often readers walk away with more new questions than they entered with.

Every expert in any subject matter I have ever interviewed declared that what gave them distinction compared to non-experts is that they had far more new questions. Humble experts practice beginner's mind. That's their power over people who think they know all there is to know.

It's a juicy paradox that more experience leads to more humility. The more we know, the more we want to know. Restricting what we know is the most certain way to live a learning-disabled life. This is true of us individually and collectively. What we know is not the problem. It's not yet having developed humility as a basic personal and social literacy.

The spirit of new questions is the realization that when we think we know things, our new questions are few. When we think there is much more to know, our new questions are many. That's humility in practice. This simple wisdom has application for anyone who is a parent, spouse, teacher or leader. Particularly in times of unprecedented uncertainty, our greatest gift to them is the gift of our humility.

More questions, better questions

When we want to get beyond old questions, we start with more questions.

In stuck communities that I work with, people struggle with old questions. What's wrong with this community? Why do we lack strong leaders? Why are so many people apathetic or disengaged? Why do good people leave and unwelcome people come? How can we get more funding to fix these problems once and for all?

These old questions lead to hours of vetting the same opinions, the same conclusions, the same stories, the same beliefs. As much as people give lip service to change, nothing new happens. No expert reports nor presentations on beliefs or facts that answer old questions have the power to make things otherwise. In a world of old questions, being right is our only shared achievement.

Things start to shift when we ask people what else they wonder about. We ask new questions about what they dream and how they could learn their way into these dreams. We invite them to do something they've never done collectively before. We ask them to translate everything that comes up in these conversations into new questions.

New things happen for the benefit of the complex whole. What's most interesting is that this requires no new training or funding. It starts simply with those who show up. The small group has always been the most powerful media for catalytic change.

New questions naturally emerge in the space of expanding questions. No matter how energizing or enervating a question feels, looking for more questions from the original question takes us into a larger space of possibilities. Generating more questions is infinitely more effective than trying to generate more ideas.

This happens on every level. When we struggle with anything, which is usually from an old question, we gain new clarity and traction when we entertain other questions. More questions of any kind lead to better questions every time. It's sometimes our third, fifth or ninth additional question that starts to break through to new perspectives.

Not all questions are equal

When it comes to the potential of new questions, not all are equal. Some have more potential to lead us toward new perspectives,

One of the most limiting habits in the art of questions is to judge a question at face value. This is mindlessly judging a question as immediately good or bad. Some people are instantly suspicious of new questions. Old questions seem more familiar because they are. They are the devil we know.

In many meetings I attend, certainly none that I lead, there are still leader-set agendas, which give people at least implicit permission to instantly judge and reject competing questions as wrong, even new ones which would have more ability to lead to new perspectives than old questions dominating agendas.

The potential value of any new question is unpredictable. We know that old questions by design can only lead to old answers.

Questions thrive or die on the vine of how we respond to them. Questions to which we respond with respectful appreciation and humble curiosity do better than those that are met with instant criticism, rejection and attacks.

What appears on the surface to be a good question can lead us nowhere new. Even though they generate instant interest and conclusions, some questions are not actionable.

Questions that beg for prediction and speculation often fall into the nonactionable category. These are often speculative and thinly disguised assessments and conclusions seeking conversions or affirmations.

All they do is make us feel stuck, inadequate or anxious. They don't lead to new kinds of reflection, research, learning, improvisation or mastery.

The only way to know a question's potential is to talk and think it through, learn from it, try it out and see where it leads.

Old questions, disguised

Old questions can take on new forms, remaining at their core old questions, with all the power of old questions.

How do we get more likes, followers and friends? How do we collect more things that make us look better? What is the latest gossip? What should we worry about when it comes to our children? To what ideology or theology should we pledge our allegiance? How do we stay suspicious about people whose stories we don't yet know?

As much as these have allure that can engage millions of people and screens full of pundits in clique-rich conversations, they are old questions, incapable of giving us new perspectives or deeper understanding of ourselves, each other and our world.

Once upon a time, they perhaps did. Today, they are old questions disguised as new. Pretending or insisting they are urgent doesn't make them new. Because a question is relevant doesn't necessarily make it new.

If we go through any conversation, day or week with more questions than new perspectives, it is evidence that even though they might feel new, our questions are actually old questions. If we feel like our everyday consciousness, alone or shared, is more of the same old, same old, it is because we are living from old questions.

When we see the same stories played out on personal to global scales in any media, they represent people still trying to use old questions to get new outcomes. The loudest questions are usually the oldest.

Learning this distinction is a new literacy, a new competency required to create and find new questions capable of new insights, new horizons of wonder and discovery.

Questions not to answer

Gautama Buddha refused to answer speculative questions. It didn't matter how deep or urgent they seemed. His passion was helping people find better questions. He responded to speculative questions with the truth of his direct experience, or he offered better questions.

We don't have to answer every question that comes up in our consciousness or conversations. Some only have the power to keep us stuck, divided or worse. Some just add noise that obscures our access to new perspectives. Because we feel obligated or pressured to answer a question doesn't make it a useful question.

Even though we don't have to answer every question that comes to us, we can respond with other, better, even more beautiful questions.

We live in times when we are exposed to more questions in a year than our grandparents were in a lifetime. Many are old questions incapable of leading to new perspectives.

When people are at their worst, their actions are answers to bad questions that would better go unanswered. We are all at our worst when we live our answers to old, bad questions. When people are at their best, it's because their actions are answers to good questions,

People destructive to themselves or others are so because they are compelled to answer old, destructive questions instead of dedicating themselves to new ones. If they refused to answer bad questions, they would be at their best.

If we simply refuse to answer bad questions, we would create more space for new questions that would better support our success and the success of others. Our questions determine how we show up in the world. There are not good or bad people, only good or bad questions.

Beliefs

Most people, teams, organizations and communities still try to create their desired future with goals.

We have been socialized to assume that we need beliefs to create the future we want to see. Goals are statements of commitment based in all kinds of beliefs. Committing to any goal, modest or bold, requires we hold certain beliefs. Beliefs are assumptions about ourselves and our world.

The more uncertainty we experience, the lower we set our goals because of our concerns and doubts. We feel most uncertainty with goals others impose on us. One reason why things change so slowly is because we set the most risk-averse goals possible in order to prevent unbearable disappointment.

The good news is we don't need beliefs to create a new future.

I have long suggested that people frame every goal as a question. "What would it look life if...?" and "How could we...?" are two simple ways to make this translation.

When beliefs are translated into questions, questions have 3-5 times more power and possibility than statements of belief. When I ask people how questions feel, they express feeling inspired, energized and engaged. They are far more willing to take on more courageous questions than tentative goals.

Reality is, no matter how many goals we commit to, the future remains intrinsically unknowable. Even the most carefully detailed goals don't create a more knowable future.

Creating a new future together doesn't necessary mean we need new beliefs but simply new questions. When people in communities move into flourishing together, it's not because they commit to beliefs. It's because they join together in new questions.

We see an emerging body of stories today about people in communities thriving side by side without having first changing their own or each other's beliefs, only their shared new questions.

They are starting schools where young women for the first time can be safely educated into a future where they share human rights with other young women around the world. They are filling public spaces in neighborhoods and villages with shared gardens. They are networking students to start new businesses before graduation. They are liberating villages from utility and tax bills with net energy creation. They are sharing kitchens, tools, technologies and child care in new flourishing communities.

In each case, it is new questions not beliefs that created the inventive collaborations that made the difference.

Vulnerable beliefs

Beliefs live on a continuum from venerable to vulnerable.

We don't question venerable beliefs. Without definitive evidence for them, we know they are true simply because they feel true to us. The more others we trust feel they're true, the more venerable they become. Beliefs tend to become more venerable with age. They are often answers to old questions.

They get stronger any time others try to talk us out of them in a war of facts, logic or weapons.

Venerable beliefs don't have to have any objective validity. They can defy data, logic and even our own good or the good of others. They just have to deliver some kind of payoff for us, in this life or a next. Many virtuous behaviors and destructive addictions are based in venerable beliefs.

Vulnerable beliefs are those we begin to question. They can be beliefs that we think are not in our best interest or aligned with our deepest desires or highest good. Beliefs can move from venerable to vulnerable when new questions come up for us.

I have coached many leaders who were leaders no one wanted to work with. Because of their venerable beliefs that teams are basically untrustworthy, they defined leadership as varieties of bullying. Feeling untrusted and bullied makes it difficult for most people to work with creativity, courage, passion and engagement.

In no case did I ask or demand them to change their beliefs. We surfaced the old questions beneath their beliefs so they could finally discover the life-shaping questions behind their old beliefs and behaviors.

In each case, new questions moved them to new perspectives. As they began to live new questions about what being trustworthy and trusting could look like, they became less disabled by dysfunctional venerable beliefs. The more they entrusted and supported their teams, in the smallest of steps, the more trustworthy and trusting their teams became. They became leaders many wanted to work with.

Each story of transformation is a story of venerable unhelpful beliefs becoming helpfully vulnerable in the face of new questions, giving way to breakthroughs that change people's lives.

Deep questions

If we want a deeper understanding of ourselves, each other or our world, we only need to discover the questions that shape us. Behind everything we do and believe are questions, some that we're aware of and some we're not. When we consider any parts of our lives that are and aren't working, it's because of the questions we live from.

It's a new perspective to consider that perhaps our life works when we work from good questions and we struggle when we work from bad questions. When we change our questions, we change our lives. This is true for each of us on the planet.

Good or bad, new or old, we experience the questions that shape us on two dimensions, surface and deep.

Surface questions are those that show up in the awareness of our everyday consciousness. They are the ones we ask ourselves and each other every day. They are the ones that get us up in the morning and keep us awake at night and in meetings.

On any given day we wonder about the best uses of our time, the shortest distances between destinations, why people act as they do and how to proceed at a fork in the road.

Deep questions live beneath our awareness in the dynamic space of our deep mind. They are questions about the meaning of our life, our personal narrative, what we believe, value and dream.

Our awareness has the ability to process about 50 bits of information per second. That's our capacity for conscious awareness, what we know we know at any moment in time.

Beneath this awareness, our deeper mind, a network of trillions of neurons, processes 10 million bits of information per second. What we're consciously thinking in any given moment of our lives represents roughly .000005 of all the thinking going on in our whole mind that includes our awareness and deep mind.

It is the whole that makes us who we are. We are what the whole is doing from one fresh moment to the next.

As long as our deep questions remain outside our awareness, we do not have choice about them. When we become aware of them, we have choice about them.

We can know our deep, life shaping questions through knowing our conscious beliefs. Each belief an answer to organizing deep questions.

I have long held the belief that everyone on the planet has the ability to learn. This belief is an answer to several questions.

Can everyone really learn at any point in their life, regardless of circumstances? Can I teach people to learn what they would be surprised to learn? Is it fair for me to expect people to learn? If people don't learn, is it more about the teaching method than the learner?

I would easily admit that these have shaped the passion and arc of my career and life. If they don't work for me anymore, if I don't feel energized by them, I now have the choice to discover and create new questions that would. Knowing these are my deep life questions, I can alter them in ways that become more relevant and richer.

By reflecting on what kinds of questions our beliefs could answer, we discover our deep questions. We are then at choice with them. We can decide whether to keep living by them or create new questions to live by.

When we want a deeper understanding ourselves or anyone, all we have to do is know the questions that shape our lives.

When we were young, we enjoyed watching the flows and swirls of iron filings on a sheet of paper as we moved a magnet around below the paper. This is how questions work. Everything we think, feel, learn and do is shaped and organized by the magnetic pull of our explicit and implicit questions.

What's best is that we don't have to argue with ourselves or anyone about any of what we believe. We are at our best when we simply get new perspectives. We get new perspectives by getting new questions. We learn rather than yearn our way into a new future.

Stuckness

Part of being human is finding new ways to get stuck. Cleverly or clumsily, we dedicate whole days and nights to finding new ways to get unstuck.

When we feel stuck, we are asking ourselves old questions in honest yet futile hope for new answers. They could be questions of our own making, questions borrowed from family and friends, questions from experts or authority figures. Their origins are irrelevant to the fact of their inability to get us unstuck.

Sometimes, we have undying faith in them because we simply have created no alternative new ones.

Why me? Why do they do this? When will things get better? How can I get more time in a day? Why can't I get others to do what they're supposed to? How can I get things finally back to normal? Why don't people get that it's all about me? What else can I buy that can medicate my inconsolable sense of deficiency?

These are all old questions that are as seductive as they are unproductive. The more urgent they feel, the more we obsess over them and turn them into flies in otherwise satisfying conversational soups.

Until we get clear on the unique power of new questions, if a question feels important or valid, we feel that right answers to it hold the key to our future wellbeing and success. We don't realize how we are complicit in our own stuckness through loyalty to old questions.

We are like people traveling across a lake by boat to explore mountains on the other side and refuse to leave the boat to explore when we get there. We have to leave old questions that served past travels well in order to discover new vistas of possibilities beyond. If any familiar question makes us feel stuck, it's likely an old question.

We get stuck in old questions and unstuck in new questions. The more we discover the power of new questions, the less faith we have in old questions that get and keep us stuck.

Simply realizing that we're trying to navigate from old questions starts the process of getting unstuck. Doubting the usefulness of old questions frees us from them. It opens space for new questions. All it takes to discover new questions is simply to stay curious for more.

How we learn to be uncurious

It's not our fault. That we could get stuck in old questions and not know how to craft new ones is testament to how we were educated.

So much of traditional education is about memorizing answers to the questions of people we believed were smarter than us.

We can go through whole cycles of education without learning how to craft different, more or new questions. Like creativity, curiosity leading to new questions dramatically declines with education.

Most employers find job applicants with boatloads of education unprepared for real work. I have met many educators who admit to having no clue what questions graduates will encounter in future work contexts. This trend is critically worse the more new questions in the workplace churn with ever-increasing frequency and complexity.

Answer-centered pedagogy disincentivizes curiosity as a fail. Exams are constructed and governed for old answers rather than new questions. Industrial education was specifically designed for a workplace requiring single right answer questions, with no regard for the reality that complex changing contexts require different and better questions, not better answers to old, unadapted questions.

It is a system defining learning as memorizing that excelled in preparing us to be impatient and surface-obsessed. Graduates of these systems grow up without strengths in creative and critical thinking as employees and citizens.

Our parents and teachers held themselves as arbiters of questions, expecting us to consider theirs most worthy of attention and loyalty.

In all the years I taught leadership in graduate business schools, I used a question-based approach. Each class session had set topics I promised to deliver on. Students generated new learning from secondary research they did from new questions they developed on the assigned topics.

These were talented mid level managers and business owners in large corporations seeking to accelerate their careers with an Executive MBA.

As most were graduates of high ranked colleges, they were largely unprepared for the assignment to identify their new learning questions. It would take the first few weeks and assignments to guide them in this new skill set.

They were still accustomed to being disengaged. They were still herded into meetings and trainings where information was pushed through lectures, presentations and assigned readings. If time permitted, they could raise their questions at the end.

Never did the promise of value depend on the quality of their questions and the rigor of their discovery.

They caught on to what it means to be a relentless, question-based learner and their lives were forever changed. I would see them years later explaining how those lessons transformed their lives, with abundant stories of evidence.

The Nature of Questions

Our relationship to uncertainty

We can't plan uncertainty away. Plans are assumptions. When we want to know how predictable our world is all we need to do is make a plan. Our most intelligent plans are agile plans. The more connected our world becomes, the more unpredictable it becomes.

Uncertainty is more a gift or problem. When we see uncertainty more as gift, our life is about learning. It is more about discovering what we don't know than defending what we do. There is so much to learn. Learning is about mystery and mastery.

When our relationship to uncertainty is learning, every day is a gift. Every situation is a treasure. The only failure is the failure to learn.

After decades of writing, teaching and being engaged as expert with people all over the world, it's amazing to me every day how much more I have to learn. There is so much about the world I don't know. No amount of accelerating my own learning could keep up with even a fraction of the world's acceleration.

There are so many mysteries to plumb, so many stories I have yet to savor, so many beautiful people I have yet to meet and know. Every new article I stumble on opens new doors of questions, new windows of wonder.

When our passion is learning, surprise is a friend and teacher. We understand that the best things in life happen unplanned. We enjoy strangers for the possibility of delightful serendipity they represent. We enjoy new places to visit, new music to hear, new art to ponder, new stories to relish, new cultures to explore, new preparations to cook.

We are more energized than exasperated by the unknown. We like to discover beyond the known. Facts interest us because they are tips of discovery icebergs.

We see our beliefs as lenses rather than predictions. They don't preempt our appetite for curiosity. We live with a deeper fondness for new questions than old answers.

The more we know, the more we realize we don't know and even more profoundly, suspect there are always more things we don't even know we don't know. We live at an epistemological crossroads, realizing that to survive and thrive we need to reinvent how we know ourselves, each other and our world. We are more interested in being explorers than explainers.

Being right

Because feeling right releases reward chemicals in our brain, it can be a significant source of happiness.

One of the most interesting aspects of feeling right is that we can feel right without being right. While feeling right, it is impossible to know we're wrong, even when we're completely wrong. We don't know what we don't know. This happens on any scale. One person, dozens or millions of people can be wrong without knowing they are.

When we feel right, we aren't aware of any deficiencies or flaws in our thinking. Everything we we know, we know is true. It takes some kind of outside evidence or question to know or suspect we're actually wrong.

Even though I grew up rewarded for being right, I have learned to relish the wisdom of being wrong. Each moment of discovering a wrong assumption is an opportunity to seek new clarity in uncertainty.

It's interesting to reflect on times in our lives we discovered we were wrong. Before we reallze we were wrong, we only felt right.

This explains our frustration with people we know are wrong and who don't know they are. They can't. No one can. It's not a character flaw or personality defect. It's how human brains work.

One way to get beyond being right, and possibly discovering we could be wrong, is to welcome new questions about our own beliefs.

Is this really true? Is it always true? Are there exceptions? Is there any part of it that could be not true? Could the opposite also be true in some ways? Could someone with a different perspective have a valid story? What questions does this belief answer and what other questions could we have?

Just knowing we could be wrong without knowing it opens us to the possibilities of being more flexibly humble than obnoxiously right.

Certainty, the addiction

The human brain is hardwired for addiction. It has the ability to be addicted to many chemical substances. Certainty is a chemical substance. We can become addicted to certainty.

Certainty addiction has many possible origins. We experience earthly shame and punishment for not knowing answers to imposed questions. We are socialized to believe that eternal shame and punishment would befall those doubting venerable communal dogmas. We discover that we could get the advantage over others if we were more right.

When we are addicted to certainty, even though we can appear cool and in control, we live with chronic unease. We're ever vigilant that there might be something we don't know. Having endless access to people and information feeds our insecurity until we wonder if certainty doesn't need to be a requirement for a meaningful life, productive work or thriving communities.

The more adept I became at living from new questions, the more I learned to believe that I could accomplish all kinds of things while uncertain. Simply guided by new questions, I finished degrees, started businesses, wrote books, worked in unfamiliar cultures, survived near death experiences, took on new talents, languages and passions with significant uncertainties.

Every new challenge is an opportunity to do well even while uncertain. Every new job we take, every new trip we embark on, every new book we begin, every new project we start, every new relationship we enter are vast spaces of uncertainty that we navigate well with new questions.

We enjoy the way, one question at a time. We discover that uncertainty can be a boundless playground for connecting, learning and growing.

The way of intuition

When it comes to living new questions, we have two ways of discovery: inquiry and intuition. Inquiry is action; intuition is reflection.

In the discovery of inquiry, we pose questions to others and searches online. We try something out. We improvise and experiment.

In the discovery of intuition, we extract new insights from sensing patterns and connecting dots in new ways. Many of our best new questions require intuition for insights.

Below everyday awareness, there is a complex and adaptive deep mind that is millions of times more engaged than our awareness in thinking, reflecting and sense making, moving us over and over from uncertainty to clarity.

Within our deeper mind is our intuition. This is our inner wisdom. It can know things beyond what our awareness can even imagine. Where our awareness feels distinct and separate from the rest of the world, deep mind feels seamlessly connected to everything else. It has access to knowing patterns before our awareness knows them.

Intuition speaks in a soft voice. We hear it when we quiet awareness. Quieting awareness happens when we are mindfully present. It can happen in nature, meditation and any flow experience that creates a clear, calm awareness.

Living from old questions with their instant, certain answers prevents the growth of our ability to tap into our intuition. Using intuition to answer new questions accelerates this growth. Just having more new questions nurtures this growth.

When we live more from intuition, we anticipate changes and opportunities as never before. Our sense of timing improves. We enjoy increasingly more complex questions. We can see patterns in large and dynamic amounts of information. We are less fooled.

Assuming our way into the future

Assumptions are answers to old questions in the absence of facts. They feel true. We include them in what we know. They are proxies for certainty.

I learned to assume all manner of things about people in countries and cultures I never personally or directly explored. Many times, I borrowed these assumptions from trusted others. Eventually living and working with these people from distant lands revealed layers of inaccuracies in these borrowed assumptions.

We've entered an age of fake news and truth hacks. Anyone with a charged phone can propagate false content on any open platform. Commercial media companies and political leaders and groups can publish whatever serves their financial agendas with the intent to deceive and manipulate perception, opinion and ultimately action.

When we know how to question assumptions we are open to other possibilities. We are free from misinformation and our own self-limiting beliefs.

This conversation opens the door to question what we mean by facts in the first place. Reality is always larger than facts because reality includes what we consider as facts and everything related that we don't yet fully know, understand or comprehend. Reality includes all relevant knowns and unknowns.

Facts are seductive to the mind that doesn't yet hold the distinction between reality and fact. It is this distinction that speaks to the saying that there is nothing as unpredictable as the past.

Do we really need beliefs?

Before we discover we can navigate any kinds of uncertainties with new questions we need beliefs to manage life's constant of unknowns. Our beliefs are our navigational systems guiding us through life's daily uncertainties.

There's nothing wrong with beliefs. When we're young, we ingest all kinds of beliefs from our families, teachers and friends. They guided us in how to think, feel, act and decide. Over time, they became intrinsic to our narrative.

In my youth I was fascinated with creatives like artists and inventors. I couldn't get enough time studying them. I believed that they, like many people I admired, had unique qualities and powers I didn't and would possibly never have in this lifetime.

This belief was my answer to the old question about what I lacked that they had. This belief directly shaped how I limited my own creativity, even though I felt great passion for it.

Years later, in developing my first book, I researched artists and inventors close up. I did so from endless questions to them about their experience, process and consciousness. I discovered how many strengths and passions they had in common and most unexpectedly that I shared with them as well.

Guided by my new questions, I no longer needed my beliefs to make sense of creativity, them and myself. This set off a whole unfolding of new questions about my own creativity that launched the creativity of my rich writing career two decades ago.

The more we learn to live from new questions the less we need the guidance of beliefs.

When I did a global study on happiness for a book four years ago, I went into it with a variety of new questions that resulted in making my life-long beliefs about happiness less necessary. I discovered a whole new level of happiness from new questions.

When we live from new questions we don't have to make enemies of those with different beliefs. We don't have to waste valuable time trying to make sense of fake news.

We don't have to change our beliefs, including those that are self-defeating and wrong. We can believe whatever we want. We enjoy new possibilities through new questions.

New questions can lead to deepening, growing and refreshing our beliefs.

Seductive questions

Each new generation of adults socializes each next generation of children with the old questions. It's been this way for eons.

Children who grow up to be peaceful and connected adults are raised by questions about peace. Their peers who grow up to be violent or isolated adults are raised by questions about violence and isolation.

Fortunately the global trend in the last thousand years, even punctuated recently by the appearances of greater violence, has been toward more peace.

Out of trust, children take the gravitas of parental questions seriously. They pretend, then sincerely believe, that their survival and success depends on answering them correctly.

These are the questions of sincere care and vulnerability in the face of uncertainty. Do you understand what's best for you? Do you know how much we worry? What were you thinking? Each is a classic old question that never had the power to provoke new perspectives.

By proxy we do the same with the questions of teachers and bosses. Only when we understand the distinction between old and new questions do we let go of blind loyalty to old questions. We become capable of new questions.

New questions do not signal disrespect. We can have deep respect for the inquiry traditions of our foremothers and forefathers and still welcome new questions they could not anticipate much less imagine.

Growth mindsets

Each of us lives more from a growth or fixed mindset. A growth mindset is knowing we can change, that we can learn and master different ways of being and interacting in our world.

A fixed mindset is knowing we can't change. We are what we are. In a fixed mindset world, life is about finding others who will reward, or at least tolerate, us for being who we are without change.

The idea of a fixed mindset is an old belief. We now know from neuroscience that there are in fact no permanent structures in our brain. We can rewire our brains with new habits at any point in our lives. We are not confined in any way to who we have been.

This opens up all kinds of new questions about what new habits of thinking and doing we would most want to grow and enjoy.

When I was young my teachers would remind us that we have so much more potential. It got us wondering how much potential we had that we didn't even know possible. It sparked a growth mindset that would illuminate so many new questions about what we could do that we hadn't yet done. It empowered us to dream impossible dreams.

A fixed mindset is a useful belief when we have low tolerance for uncertainty. Part of this mindset is the belief that changing anything about ourselves will increase the probabilities of unwelcome and intolerable uncertainty.

The more we welcome, if not value, uncertainty as learning opportunity, the more we are able to live from a growth mindset. More of our questions are new questions.

Until someone migrates toward a growth mindset, expecting, asking or supporting their change is an unrealistic endeavor, however desperate or well-intended our efforts.

What helps is engaging them in more new questions, about anything, especially in areas where they don't have fixed, colonistic or defensive beliefs.

Perspectives

Perspective is focus. We spend more time thinking about deficiencies or strengths, our own and those of others.

The deficiency focus is seductive. This is focus on old questions about what we lack, what's wrong, what we're failing to do. There are always deficiencies. People who crave control keep us focused on them.

They distract us from our goodness and the possibilities of creating an abundance perspective for goodness for all.

In an abundance perspective, we wonder what would bring everyone peace. We wonder what would help people contribute peace to others.

What would peace for all look like? How could we bring more peace to ourselves and others? These are abundance perspectives.

When we come from an abundance perspective we are not confused or distracted by fake news, which typically focuses on what's wrong, what's deficient. We are not seduced by stories of who most disappoints us, who we could blame for deficiencies. We do not get stuck in old questions.

When I received my African name, Sekou, meaning wise man, the elder women of my welcoming community took me aside to narrate hours on the history of slavery in America I never imagined. Growing up, I had no exposure to this, given what our education authorities referred to as "American History."

I have since been incapable of viewing the dynamics and impacts of slavery in the same way. My perspective shifted forever. The experience raised more new questions than a lifetime could explore. It humbled me into realizing how limited my white, male, privileged perspective was.

The experience invited me into new questions about new ventures into peace.

Exceptions and outliers

The most salient feature of beliefs is how they generalize.

In every generalization about others is the reality of those who don't fit the norm. When we become curious about exceptions and outliers, new possibilities emerge.

I have friends who work with communities of abject poverty. When they look for people who want to start their own businesses that could add new value to the community, they find them. When they support and connect their dreams, they discover how these communities could flourish as never before, defying the odds of old beliefs and old questions.

In every struggling community there are people who do not represent the expected norms. They hold the promise of new possibilities because they live new questions.

This is how it is in any group we generalize about. There are always exceptions and outliers to people we generalize based on nationality, education, career, net worth, gender and generation. In new questions we explore and expect those who don't fit predictably into our generalizations.

Delicious ambiguity

My grandparents emigrated to the US as teenagers at the beginning of the last century. It was a burst of unprecedented mobility. That mobility was nothing like it is now where people instantly intersect across time zones, making all kinds of new genres of connections possible.

One of my Italian grandfather's favorite mantras was a beautiful simplicity: "It takes all kinds to make the world go 'round." It has fed my lifelong boundless appetite to enrich my life with wonder about other cultures.

As more people share more of themselves with people dissimilar to them, more of us become cultural blends, mixes, synergies and syntheses. Socially, psychologically, religiously, spiritually, economically and technically we are moving from monocultures to polycultures.

We are weaving lives inspired by many cultures, not just those we were raised within. We are enjoying new questions about the kinds of foods, music, art, science and technologies from other cultures we can explore, appreciate and use to enrich our lives and consciousness.

We wonder how our lives can be enriched beyond the boundaries of our native geographies.

We are less bound by historical stereotypes. We are less either-or. Many new questions are questions of both-and. How could we weave the best from anywhere in the world into the rich fabric of our life? How could we create new fusions of everyday life that draw from the best of any cultures? How can our kitchen creations, spiritual rituals, playlists and friends represent rich varieties? These are the new questions inspiring new ambiguities.

When people don't want deeper understanding

There are people who are content with surface understanding of themselves, others and their world. Surface understanding is uncomplicated. No new questions are required. A sense of certainty is maintained. It's a life of cliches.

When we live from surface understanding, we believe we can manage any of life's uncertainties relying on what we already know, largely uninterested in the curiosity of new questions.

Life is an unfolding of new uncertainties. Each new chapter in our narrative begins with new uncertainties.

Navigating each successfully takes deeper understanding of ourselves, each other and our world.

As much as we need deeper understanding at these transitions, not everyone wants it. Some people see deeper understanding as a potential disruption to their surface understanding of things, their beliefs about what's right, their addiction to certainty. What they are right about is that seeking deeper understanding means exposing ourselves to uncertainty, for which they have low tolerance.

There are four basic reasons why anyone would resist deeper understanding of anything.

Knowing more can lead to feeling more responsible and potentially more guilt. Knowing more can lead to feeling less condemning, and potentially more compassion for the intolerable. Knowing more can lead to questioning ourselves and potentially eroding unconditional self confidence. Knowing more can lead to unmanageable uncertainty, potentially threatening an addiction to being right.

To want deeper understanding we need new questions. We need questions about what's knowable beyond what we know.

We seek deeper understanding of anything when we realize we don't have to disturb, disregard or deny our beliefs, we just need to have new questions.

The gift of skepticism

When it comes to old questions, skepticism signals disloyalty and disruption. In new questions, it opens the lens of wonder.

Wonder is opening to what else could be possible. It leads to a place of clarity as alternative to certainty. We don't cling to clarity the way we do with certainty. In clarity, we hold our truths as lenses rather locations. We create space to know more.

People with skepticism are gifts to be engaged rather than problems to be solved. When we no longer fear new questions, we live with wonder rather than defensiveness and reaction. We listen. We are no longer divided in opposition but rather connected in curiosity.

Skepticism is seeing things for ourselves. It's not that we don't trust the views of trusted others. It's that we delight in the journey ignited by new questions. We question our own allegiance to what prevents our own learning.

We are no longer enemies of the future but co-creators of the future we together want to see. We realize more of our potential. We become less complacent and complicit in legacies we would more likely morn than celebrate.

Skepticism isn't opposing views. It's not polemical. It's wondering beyond the surface. It's the realization of our humility.

Shutting down skepticism, our own or that of others, is its own form of learning disability. The only way to deeper understanding of anything perplexing or sacred to us is through putting no limits on our questions.

Learning questions

As much as we might work tirelessly to create a predictable future for ourselves and those we care about, life presents us with what we categorize as challenges. They could be things we have longed for and those we have loathed to happen.

We are challenged by our work, our children and families, by politics, change and problems of all kinds.

Challenges are intrinsically spaces of uncertainty. The scope of any challenge is equal to the scope of its uncertainty. When we successfully navigate challenges, it's when we learn our way into a new future.

One question that transforms the perspiration of challenge into the inspiration of learning is: What can I learn here that would help me navigate this challenge?

If there are people who have successfully navigated this kind of challenge, we gain immeasurably from discovering what they learned, expectedly and unexpectedly, in the process of moving from uncertainty to success.

This begins with identifying our learning questions. What do we want to understand that we don't know today? What do we want to be able to do that we don't know how to do today? What do we want to learn how to feel more?

Any question that represents curiosity for new learning energizes us to learn our way into the future we would most like to see.

A better self

There are two attitudes toward seeking a better self.

One is that it's not necessary. This ancient perspective derives from a belief that our life would be better if everyone else grew a better self. All of our questions are about how we can make this more possible.

The other is that a better self is key to our success and survival. How we are now will not cut it. This perspective derives from an old belief that, however good we might be, we are not good enough if we want a future different from the past.

Self-improvement continues to be a multi-billion dollar industry, significantly fueled by old questions about how we can become different than we are today.

These are questions about what's wrong with us, what we're lacking, why we get in our own way, why bad things keep happening despite our best planning and efforts, why people make things more difficult than they should be and what we can do to change them.

As old questions, it's unlikely they will lead to new perspectives. For that, we need new questions.

New questions are questions about what's already good about us and what we dream for ourselves, each other and our world. It's questions about what new habits we want to grow and how new habits grow. It's questions about what we did to bring about our progress, success and luck in our life so far and how we can use those lessons to present challenges.

The new questions are about cultivating deeper understanding about how we unknowingly bring about our own happiness, success and growth. Each of us have had moments of these in our lives and yet didn't explore with new questions how we brought them about.

When we do, we realize our power and create more moments of happiness, success and growth.

Looking good

We have become a performance obsessed society where the pinnacle of success is looking good in any ways we can. This emanates from the old questions of materialism where we measure the meaning of our lives in units of consumption and collection.

We want to look good in how we manage our brand, time, assets, friendships, families and careers.

We now have ways to keep up to the minute on how people look good across life's dimensions. It's called social media.

We know we are living by the old questions of how to look good if we spend time on social media wandering with a sense of personal deficiency in the spiritual deserts of endless comparisons.

This obsession is caffeinated by a host of old questions. Who's doing better than us? What are other people achieving that we haven't yet?

Where are falling behind? What are we lacking? How can we manage the stress of all this better? Why aren't we managing the stress of all this better?

One alternative to the self-induced pressure of looking good is the new question of how we can improvise a purpose-based life based on contributing goodness to our world. A life of meaning is a life of being more contributor than consumer. This begins with a different set of questions than the old self-serving ones.

What good could we do in our world? Where is good needed right now? In what small ways can we begin? Are there people we could also invite into this?

Contributors live longer lives of meaning, no matter what challenges and uncertainties they endure and thrive from.

The new normal

One of the classic risk aversion questions is: Is that normal?

Normal is an elusive principle, varying by geography and demography. It's an old question designed to keep us inside the invisible fences of what is acceptable to the most critical among us. It's questions about compliance. What will earn approval of those whose approval is required or desired? What does it mean to belong?

Unique is fast becoming the new norm. Difference is the new normal, setting off an avalanche of new question possibilities. What unique expressions of not normal would have value in our communities, workplaces and schools? What are the costs of normal; what opportunities and perspectives do we lose?

On some days, our choice is to be normal or new. Normal questions are often the old questions. New questions do not require approval to have power. They don't have to be popular or trending. They are often on the edges of the norm.

In the realms of human experience, normal isn't always thriving, especially when uncertainty is the new norm. When life presents us with a choice between being normal or thriving, we can wonder how thriving might be our preference.

The World of Questions

Education

If we accept the premise that our life is shaped by our questions, the purpose of education would be to teach people how to create and pursue new questions.

Public education is a relatively recent experiment in the history of human experience, beginning in the early days of the industrial revolution when farmers brought their families to work in cities and their children left behind their daily engagement on farms.

Even though we live in a profoundly different world, we still have schools that not only don't teach the art of questions, they prevent it with an answer-based approach to learning.

Having a world of answers literally at our fingertips makes it more possible for all education to be question-based.

Regardless of their economic or cultural context, living from new questions is not something children need to learn. Self-organized curiosity is hard wired into them. All schools can do is help them develop or forget this capacity. The most advanced schools dedicate their efforts to helping learners learn new strategies for forming and going about new questions.

Workplaces and communities that thrive in the future will have members prepared by schools that taught them the literacy of new questions.

Every smart team on the planet today attracts and retains avid learners. They are valued as creative, current and resilient. Every smart community values members who have passion for learning new things that drive new contributions to the community. Every smart relationship engages people who are constant learning companions in ways that keep their shared space continuously fresh and vital.

This takes a transition from old questions about education. How do we base graduation on memorizing information (that is now on every smart phone or watch)? How do we get students to comply with what governing bodies command as curriculum rather than rather learn what they're passionate about and what would serve their communities?

What would it look like to teach learners how to form and work from new questions that can help them read, search, interview, observe, discover, improvise, create and succeed in every dimension of their lives?

New questions take a different approach. What questions do learners bring to the learning table? What community projects and efforts could be used as a basis for question-based learning in area of learning vital to future work, life and citizenship?

At work

When teams at work struggle, they work from old questions they deem valid and vital to their survival and success. These are often questions imposed by their leaders, inherited from their academic pursuits and proposed by the latest thought leader fashions in mainstream business magazines.

Teams do better with new questions. This is the transition from old questions about how to manage wasteful meetings and emails to what apps we could engage that would eliminate these in the first place.

It's moving from old questions about how to manage tensions to how to form mutual agreements that could make these less inevitable. It's migrating from old questions about what kind of leadership people need to how people can act empowered with new habits and norms of integrity, initiative and inclusion.

These are the new questions that replace old questions that were designed for an age that barely resembles this. The imperative to get better at framing new and better questions is in no small part inspired by what could be the future of work.

In the future of work, much of what constituted work in the last hundred years will become unnecessary in the next. Powered by all manner of artificial intelligence and the internet of things, many white and blue collar jobs will be no longer required. This includes jobs related to medicine, law, government, education, manufacturing and transportation. Even jobs in service sectors will shift in a growing sharing economy.

The old questions will not prepare us for these new uncertainties. When we reinvent work to me more meaningful in the future of work, it will be because we get our questions right.

The nature of work today still heavily resembles the industrial era influenced by management theories assuming that people work best when all of their thinking is designed out of work by instituting bosses, policies, procedures, role and job descriptions and fear-based systems of accountability consequences. These were based on old questions about what we do with people who can't be trusted to think.

Every organization trying to perpetuate these questions has the highest levels of disengagement on the planet.

Those with the highest levels of engagement are operating from a completely different set of questions.

How can we build organizational cultures where people feel free to interact at their best? How do we help teams become smarter and more nimble? These are producing completely different levels of results, including empowering people with growth that helps them succeed at home and in their communities.

Experts

At lunch a few years ago with a friend who teaches doctoral nursing students, a mystery unraveled for me. Why do so many medical studies with all the requisite peer reviews and empirical validations contradict each other?

Details get lost in marketing. We find out that this drug sometimes works and sometimes doesn't. It depends on which studies you follow, which commercials you watch.

When we look into the details, we find that this drug has these promised prime and side effects with a specific demographic like mid-aged African-American women with a history of high blood pressure and diet deficiencies in certain mineral protocols. Only recently have experts used women in studies for women's medicine.

In the Industrial Age, we were schooled in loyalty to whoever our authorities positioned as the experts. We were rewarded for not questioning what experts declared as fact or reality, no matter how many new unresearched questions we had.

Above all, we learned to believe that their questions were the most important. We learned to have less faith in ourselves and each other when it came to new or better questions in any field or pursuit.

Everyone at the top of their fields I have ever interviewed prefer to talk more about expertise than experts. They confess that what distinguishes them with unique value is the fact that they have more new questions than others in their fields. They are more open to new possibilities and perspectives than others.

If we want to be passionate learners, we can no longer outsource our curiosity to the answers of people positioned or advertised as experts.

Because we are inspired by someone's brilliant television or stage appearance doesn't mean it's wise to let their sage answers preclude our fresh questions. If anything, the more experts emerge in our media of choice, the more sources of inspiration we have for new questions.

Growing a business

The average company today has the lifespan of sheep. With all due respect to these ruminants, it's curious how an organization with all manner of brains, budgets and brands could have the longevity of lambs.

When graduate students do post mortem case studies on top shelf businesses that barely last 10-15 years, they reveal clear patterns. These organizations operated from beliefs bolstered by old questions. They worked from the wrong questions.

The old questions still seem reasonable, if not vital. How can we protect our brand, markets and talent? How can we avoid investments that take longer than a quarter to harvest? How can we grow by acquisition that will expand what we're already doing?

How can we stick to the knitting? How can we continue to leverage fear to keep people and suppliers under control? How can we get the world to understand us, adapt to us and reward what we as experts believe it needs?

There is nothing necessarily wrong with the old questions if we're in a fairly predictable world. The old questions were designed for times of greater certainties. In a time of greater uncertainty, only new questions will support our success and sustainability.

Companies that thrive for decades and centuries longer operate from a different set of questions.

How can we surprise the imagination of markets? What if we focused more on our people's passions and strengths than on their weaknesses and deficiencies? How can we keep all of our planning agile? How do we distribute governance?

How could we grow thriving cultures that become key to the success of good strategies and structures? What are the new questions inviting us to dream with more courage?

There is a reason there are over 5,000 companies today over 200 years old. It's their culture of asking and living new questions.

Entrepreneurship

It is becoming more apparent, and the evidence supports the reality, that new scales of work and value do not come about by big anything: big business, big banks or big governments. They come about because of entrepreneurs whose passion is new questions about solving real problems people enjoy rewarding. It's been this way for a long time.

The value they create and deliver results from countless new questions. They believe in the magical intersection of serendipity and usefulness. Their questions begin in compassion.

What do people struggle with? What are the margins of opportunity neglected by those whose profit demands require attention to larger pursuits?

More often than not, innovating entrepreneurs create breakthroughs outside of their fields. This is the power of new questions.

The more communities move from old questions about how to graduate more employees to new questions about how to incubate more entrepreneurs, the more they will thrive.

The old questions were about what we want to be when we grow up and what jobs we wanted to pursue. The new ones are about what our dreams are and what problems we want to help solve.

There is a large landscape of mythology about why startups fail and succeed. We talk about factors like idea, timing, investing and managing.

All of my experiences doing and coaching startups, along with those of close serial entrepreneur friends, point to the observation that successful startups are successions of new questions. We thrive when we do not make uncertainty the enemy, but rather our most cherished gift. We progress one new question at a time.

The sharing economy

In the most improbable ways, some of the fastest growing companies around are booking rooms and rides without owning lodging or cars. They are leveraging peer to peer trust through transparency so people with personal lodging and cars can share them with others.

Neighborhoods are launching libraries of things where people can borrow everyday tools, appliances and resources they would use for maybe a few hours a year if owned. Organizations are establishing vibrant virtual spaces where people can learn more from each other in real time than they could from countless scheduled classes and conferences they can't afford the time to attend.

As social learning replaces formal learning, people naturally develop their literacy for new questions.

They operate from new questions. How could we create the kind of mutual trust that allows people to share what they have for mutual benefit? What other forms of trade might be possible from this model?

What are the possibilities of barter and time share economies? These are new questions transforming the way we think about being local and global citizens and how to grow economies powered by social capital.

Technology

Every day, there are countless innovators working overtime to make life better by bringing new technologies to life. They work outside the walls of institutions. They seek scale and spread. They are relentless in their passion to solve problems and realize dreams as never before.

The promise of technology is to give more people affordable access to an unpredictable universe of things that can make life better for all.

Technology democratizes new breakthroughs in medicine, social connections, knowledge and know how sharing, peer to peer currencies, literacies, direct engagement in governance and transparencies, personalized production, food and environmental justice, to name just a few categorical possibilities.

Each instance and iteration emerges from new questions, new perspectives. Many breakthroughs are flourishing children of a single mother question: "What if...?"

What if every village and neighborhood in the world had at least one 3D printer that could produce new ways to support clean water, building materials, medical prosthetics and supplies? What if dogs could be trained to anticipate seizures and text for timely help that saves lives? What if villages and towns in any climate could use natural energy and hydroponics to locally grow more food than they need?

These are happening because people are working with these new questions. The sky is the limit, and perhaps isn't.

The optimist-pessimist polarity

On any given issue on any table - whether the kitchen, community, executive or legislative table - there lives the tension of opposites between optimisms and pessimists.

The optimist question is: "How can things go right?"
The pessimist questions is: "How can things go
wrong?"

The old question is about how we divide in
conservatism and liberalism. As venerable as this old
question is, it does not typically lead to new
perspectives that have the power to make us smarter
together. If anything it keeps us divided in win-lose and
lose-lose conversations and outcomes.

The optimist-pessimist question has the potential to
make us smarter together because we can together
identify the possible upsides and downsides to any
proposal or prediction.

I introduced this to a large group of global leader
investors who were expert at adversarial, zero-sum
ideological weaponry and warfare. I had them take any
sticky issue and together identify the upsides and
downsides of any approach. They then developed

strategies together to optimize benefits and minimize downsides to any options on the table.

They were amazed how not only did it bring everyone on the same side of the table, it led to more intelligent and innovative possibilities and considerations.

In work sessions on team building, I've given groups decisions to simulate and ask them to approach it divided into conservatives and liberals.

They then become optimism and pessimists together, sharing both sides in the decision. They report in critique later that divided, they were actually slower and dumber together in the liberal-conservative debates.

Either-or is the only non-viable path if we wish to be smarter together. Pushing too hard in one direction creates push back from the other, into a downward spiral of stuckness for all. We are only smarter together in the curiosity space of both-and. This means working from both perspectives of optimism and pessimism, since together they represent the most realistic view approach. Neither is fully realistic.

This is what likely happens when we're smarter together because of new questions. The potential implications for the future of politics, religion and all human institutions are enormous.

Getting questions wrong in the commons

Every community, city and nation struggles with questions that devil and divide us. They are questions about rights and responsibilities, protection and trade, technology and medicine, business and economics, education and poverty, power and empowerment, welfare and warfare, alliances and adversaries, budgets and investments.

New questions create upward spirals of curiosity, learning and creativity together. If the spirals are in the opposite direction, it's often because we're working from old questions and we don't even know it's these old questions that are at the root of our downward spirals.

Even a cursory scan of questions shaping our current public and civic dialogues and debates reveals that most are old questions to begin with. Of course, the questions that represent decisions must be answered, but these decisions will be made wisely only when a whole universe of new ancillary and predecessor good questions get addressed.

Should education be public, private, both or otherwise? Should we worry about income gaps, the hoarders and homeless? What do we do with mothers who don't want their children, the children, their fathers and their communities? What should we do with political and climate immigrant families, those who have been driven from their countries by disasters and displacements? How can elected officials be entrusted and held accountable to be the smartest people in the room?

As urgent and valid as these issues are, none of these old questions have the power to move conversations forward. We need to become smarter together in discovering and crafting new questions for these issues.

This is a creative pursuit that becomes possible simply by realizing we need new questions that move us from surface to deeper understanding and from outdated to fresh perspectives.

Rethinking cities

Even enveloped in stone, metal and glass, cities are living things. As much as we have tried to engineer them, they are essentially sociological in nature. As complex adaptive systems, they grow precisely because no one is in charge.

People in elected and appointed official positions have no technical authority to engineer good people, businesses, faith communities, artists, educators, entrepreneurs or health professionals into the city, much less create the intangible conditions of their success, growth and networked collaborations.

These all happen in self-organizing ways because markets exist for them to do so and they know how to create value in these markets. People do what they have strengths, passions and opportunities to do. This all happens because people are free, not commanded to. This is how cities have grown from hundreds to hundreds of thousands and millions.

The old questions center on the flawed logic that a good city can thrive by being run the way industrial era companies have been.

How can we manage a city the way we do a corporation? How can the public hold authorities accountable for the whole? How can we sustain a system where someone rich and incompetent could run for and hold public office at any level? How can we bribe more people and businesses to come into the community and stay when they would rather leave?

New questions focus differently. How can we incubate the next generation of socially and economically responsible and competent leaders? How can leaders create more freedom for people to act from their strengths, passions and opportunities? How can network weavers do their magic in creating a more vibrant social fabric so more people are supported by others in their success? How can we grow smart cities?

One of the latest in new questions is how to launch basic income in cities where full time steady work in many industries is unreliable because companies are vulnerable to global trends and the whims of owners and political leaders to shut them down at will.

These new questions about giving people basic income and entrepreneurial competencies can breathe new life in the possibilities of entrepreneurship, gig careers and new vistas in education that are not possible when people are stuck in meaningless, less than living wage and unstable jobs and joblessness.

As new questions, they could lead to even more new questions that take us beyond basic income options.

Politics

As messy or inexplicable as politics seems, it is organized by an implicate order of questions about ancient and archetypal power beliefs. These are often old questions about which allies to build, which vulnerables to convert and which enemies to thwart. In the worst cases, they are more the questions of adolescents rather than adults.

If political questions at the table create more division and suspicion than understanding and collaboration, they are likely old questions. New questions inspire new insights into mutual interests for mutual gains. I've seen over and over around the world how people across political divides, invited to dream together, can and do.

Whether from beliefs or evidence, people at the core of political networks think they're right. They safeguard political ideologies and interpretations. At the edges, people pick and choose what they want to believe and support. When new questions are possible, they are more likely to emerge at the edges rather than cores of political networks.

Beliefs are the currencies of politics. The reason why politics doesn't always lead to better quality of life for all is that they work from the wrong questions. When we aren't clear on the new questions, we can even fund and elect people who promise to be committed to the wrong questions.

New questions in the political realm shift attention from the mutual bullying many politics contexts have come to be. They are based in the realization that in a world of spiraling interdependence, some of us cannot be winners, or losers. We win together or lose together.

One new question is about what could get to a deeper understanding. It doesn't matter what the issue, opportunity or idea. We become smarter together when we learn rather than fight our way into the future, when we move from surface to deeper perspectives.

Another new question is about who is at the table. Deeper understanding flourishes in a rich context of lenses. For any issue, who from around the world could we invite who represent technology and the arts, science and medicine, education and mediation, psychology and sociology, history and anthropology, agriculture and architecture?

The chemistries of these gifts empower the potential for new questions beyond imagination. It becomes easier to dream together the possible impossible.

Democracy and creativity

The trajectory of our lives is shaped by our questions. This is an empowering truth when we notice how our everyday questions tend to be more liberating or limiting.

On democracy, could technology advancements make more possible direct rather than representative governance? Could we have policy proposals shaped by actual subject matter experts rather than people who are not subject matter experts and have to spend most of their time in office fund raising? Could unprecedented transparency support more freedom at local rather than higher levels?

These are new questions capable of new perspectives, in contrast to old questions about how we can join or disable the enemy parties and either expand or end traditional governments.

There is an intrinsic relationship between flourishing democracies and creativity. Democracies can grow, mature and flourish to the extent that creativity grows, matures and flourishes.

On creativity, why does the research now suggest that groups of white men become smarter and more creative when women and people of color are included? Why are groups that lack guaranteed incentives and competition more creative than those that have these in abundance? Where could democracy perform better by introducing more creativity?

Are there leadership habits that help groups become more successful because of their creativity? Why does getting people to dream out at least one generation get them more creative?

We didn't have these new questions even two generations ago. Nor did we have the unprecedented levels of transformation we're seeing now with the new questions.

Until we cultivate the new literacy of forming new questions about the nature and intersections of democracy and creativity, we continue having faith in old questions, irrationally hoping for better results. The questions that gave birth to modern democracies were valid for that time, a time that had little in common with this time. Moving to more mature versions of democracy will require a whole new universe of questions.

Religion

Next to politics, religion dominates many of the organizing beliefs that shape our lives and world.

As faith networks, each religion has cores of people dedicated to protecting, preserving and promoting unquestioned dogmatic beliefs, the shoulds and whys of being human.

Each also has peripheries of people who live from the beliefs that seem most useful and mix them together for their own personal brand of religious beliefs.

Many of us do not go to religions for new questions. We go to religions of our youth, marriage or personal journey with old questions that religions are prepared to answer. Many religious beliefs are answers to old questions about should and why. How should we live? Why do things happen as they do?

Religions were a significant force in the civilization of humanity over the centuries and continue to guide people with venerable questions in living their best lives possible.

The conversation about the future of religion will be shaped by new trends.

In the US alone, fewer than 10% of Millennials, the next generation of parents, are believers in Bibles and churches. They come to the religion conversation with all kinds of new questions that aren't engaged in mainstream congregations devoutly committed to the old questions.

In times of unprecedented uncertainties, people divide into those who cling more fervently with faith in answers to old questions and those who seek new questions with little faith that old questions will help them navigate in a world difficult to predict.

There is an emerging trend across religious and non-religious lines inspired by new questions about what it means to be spiritual.

What does it mean to be connected with universal love? What does it mean to be contemplative in a busy life? What is prayer as thanks rather than asks? How is being spiritual about new ways of deeper listening?

Christianity, Judaism, Islam and Buddhism offer rich traditions of wisdom, rituals and prayer that have the power to connect us together and beyond. It is in the spiritual dimensions that new questions can bring us to new and meaningful perspectives.

Many of the over 4,000 current religions worldwide feature community and compassion in their core answers to what matters in spiritual life. We can craft all kinds of new questions about these relative to the continued and profound isolation and disconnection people feel today.

New spiritual perspectives will come from new questions about compassion and community. These are uniquely vital questions that cannot be addressed by many economic or political questions. They will play an important part of deeper understanding of the possibilities.

The need for enemies

Ancient human questions persist in every power context like politics, economics, religion and business. Who are our enemies? How can they be neutralized, colonized or obliterated?

In any conversation around the world where mention of an enemy emerges, it becomes an incredibly strong magnet attracting old questions that have no power to bring about a new future.

New questions challenge the basic premise of needing enemies. What kinds of success, progress and growth in any endeavor are possible without waging war on an enemy? If we don't vilify and scapegoat uncertainty to whose we declare as our enemies, do we become intrinsically more creative? What new potentials could we unleash if we shift our attention back from all the drama about our possible vulnerabilities?

Hundreds of studies for decades continue to indicate that in any context, competition reduces creativity because it suspends people in a state of fear. When fear is stimulated in our brain, our creativity and intelligence centers shut down.

We have mountains of evidence that all manner of art, science, technology, culture, community, compassion, healing and wisdom have come about without the requirement of an enemy. If anything, they came about through the chemistries of new collaborations.

I remember during the Cold War hearing about magnificent under the radar sharing between US and Soviet artists, scientists, educators and health care researchers.

Most of us know that we get more done together than apart. We have all kinds of examples now of global medical breakthroughs that could only be possible with collaborations among researchers who not that long ago competed against one another for credit.

This is how it is with any complex global scale questions that will continue to scale like those about disease, climate change and immigration.

How can we connect in genuine, generative and sustainable ways without being allies whose union is based on a common enemy? Could we be even better joined and served by having dreams instead of devils in common? These are new questions, capable of more fresh political and ethical perspectives than any of the old questions can.

It is terribly naive to continue believing that progress requires enemies simply because history is abundant with this narrative. It is equally unrealistic to expect that competition with enemies will make them or us smarter or better together. It will take a variety of new, more intelligent and adult questions to make new, mutually beneficial collaborations more possible.

Poverty

What people call poverty has many faces. Two billion people on the planet earn less than $2 a day. Most of these lack daily access to adequate food, water, toilets, energy, medicine and most importantly, education.

Every community in every country has people who were born into failure to thrive families. Their deepest lack is the lack of being able to imagine otherwise.

Poverty is an economic reality that often benefits many advantaged others. It is also a system of beliefs, held tightly by those on all sides of the poverty equation. Each belief is sustained by old questions, more implicit than explicit.

One emerging genre of new questions is how exceptions occur, aptly termed positive deviance. How do some children in failure to thrive neighborhoods and villages escape to schools and lives their grandparents could hardly imagine?

How do some women come together to form microfinancing collectives and microenterprises that move them and their families out of being at risk on all levels?

How are people using web enabling phones in the most remote regions to share resources in unimaginable ways? How are safe zones being expanded without violence? What motivates philanthropies that now dedicate themselves to help make all of this rather than another generation of dependencies possible?

Our curiosity about the amazing exceptions inspires more new questions and possibilities. What's most interesting is how thriving becomes more possible without overt threats to, or hope in trickling down from, the tiny network of the wealthiest people on the planet.

This perspective becomes more clear when we consider the new questions about how we can empower people without staying stuck by the old zero-sum questions.

Human rights

Whatever social class we are born into, each of us is born with the ability to learn. What we learn and become able to learn is significantly context shaped.

So much of what we become reflects what we're exposed to. People who live from new questions have no limits on what they expose themselves to. Their growth potential is unknowable.

I have friends who mentor young people in urban centers who honestly believe that learning is beyond their capabilities. Their most significant learning disability is lack of faith in their ability to learn. Even when there are potential rewards for learning, they lack self-efficacy, which puts them in a position of chronic fear in uncertainty.

Their questions are old. How can we get by with what we know? How can we make the most of our chronic dependency? How can we medicate our despair? How can we hope someone will save us? These prevents them from new perspectives.

Fear is both causal and consequential. This is the narrative of so many people when we talk about human rights.

The insidiousness of fear is that it shuts down our capacity for new questions that could otherwise inspire, support and shape new learning. The only escape from this spiral is through new questions.

Many of the old questions about human rights had to do with maneuvering more basic resources, services, technologies and work to people who lack access to these. This is very complicated work leveraging already strained economic, political, technical and infrastructure and social assets and advantages.

One compelling premise of new questions is that human rights is about education.

Considering any specific context, what kind of education would be most significant for people there - personally and collectively - and for each generation weaving the social fabric there? How can new local and visiting teachers and teaching be launched and supported? Can virtual learning be a factor? How can a focus on wellbeing and microenterprises be catalysts for new learning entry points?

The future of new conversations on human rights will feature new questions about growing local communities of learning.

Gender

In the last century, new global conversations have emerged around the question of gender and power.

Around the world, even in the largest democracies, men finally granted women the freedom to be full citizens with the ability to vote.

In many countries and cultures, men are still defending and debating old questions about how to keep women outside executive and board seats, primary child and elder care providers, subservient, uneducated or lower paid.

We are at the dawn of new considerations of gender equality. New gender questions take on a different character.

What would a world of power, responsibilities and rights sharing look like? What could men uniquely do to help support this kind of transition in sharing? What could women uniquely do? What could businesses, schools and communities do to support these new questions? The possibilities are endless. All children and elders will benefit.

The new questions imply the belief that there are certain human achievements that will only be possible if women and men are equally available for contributions to them.

What is only possible in new collaborations as partners between men and women? This is the kind of new question that will move the conversation forward.

Intimacy

Intimacy on any level isn't a given. It isn't an automatic result of falling in love, making lifelong commitments or sharing children, assets, liabilities or lives.

The question about whether intimacy should just come naturally is a very old question. It is a naive question that brings about more tension than communion.

Intimacy is an ecology of habits we learn, practice and master together. It is the result of a different set of deep questions.

Our beliefs about intimacy shape how we show up and don't, what we share and expect with our intimate others. Many of us have accumulated an impressive collection of intimacy shoulds. This is the politics of intimacy.

The old questions are many. How do we keep up with what we know or imagine to be the ideals? What do we do with all the baggage and noise that distracts us from how we want this intimacy to feel? Do we even need this intimacy? It just takes these questions to feel stuck in the intrinsic uncertainty of intimate spaces.

The new question possibilities are even greater. How do we feel most and least vulnerable? How can we share our vulnerability in ways that invoke deeper listening and feeling heard? What makes us feel most loved, cared for and cherished in an intimate space? What causes us to trust? What causes us to be trustworthy?

How can we help each other feel a larger sense of worthiness? What would it mean to be more present with each other? What if we discovered a love we never imagined before?

As these are shared, they lead to new perspectives and deeper understanding of ourselves and others. New questions create the kind of intimacy based on knowing and being known more deeply, appreciatively and mindfully.

Intimacy is as deep as our feeling heard. New questions shift us into new ways of listening. These are always more beautiful questions. We know immediately that we're living more beautiful questions because we feel immediately more beautiful together.

Growing the next generation

I commonly hear this generation of parents remark that it's not easy to predict what the world will be like when their children grow into the next generation of parents, citizens, consumers, leaders and employees.

There are some knowns. We know that this next generation will need to learn how to learn. We help when we inspire them in forming questions they can have passion about. We help when we guide them in identifying the questions behind the beliefs they inherit from us and share with their peers.

As much as we are tempted to believe we will always be smarter, if not wiser, than our children, our stories about how we learn and live from new questions will most profoundly and sustainably shape their sense of what's possible.

The challenge of developmental phases is that they always feature the tension of regressions to behaviors and attitudes from previous phases and progressions to behaviors and attitudes upcoming in next phases.

When children get stuck and perplexed by these tensions, we can help them discover and experiment with better questions.

Our prime contribution is helping them live from new questions about what it means to know, live from and grow their strengths in community with others. Their social connections will always be their greatest learning asset. They will be inspired by ours.

Family

There is a myth that as we enter each lifetime, our souls choose the families we are born into. There are further versions proposing that we come into each lifetime with specific lessons to learn and we choose the families that will most optimally make this learning possible.

Whether we subscribe to these mythologies, they can seem true.

We know the old questions about family life. Who are these people and why are some so different from each other and us? How can we try to love or at least tolerate anyone? Why could I feel closer to other people who don't even know my family than I do to some members of my family? How can I live (or without) with my family as they are?

New questions are equally possible to shape how we show up in our families. What would quality time look like with any of my family members who would be open, receptive and interested in this kind of time? What would realistic expectations of my family members look like?

Who in my life outside my family feels like my tribe and what would quality time with them look like? What personal and shared stories could we share that would help us know, understand and appreciate our personal and shared histories together?

What's clear is that like intimacy, quality family connections are not givens. We have to learn our way into them together. It takes new questions, new improvisations and new conversations.

Overwhelm

From a sense of duty, fear, guilt, greed or any cocktail of motivations, some of us on a daily basis say yes to more than we have capacity to deliver. We try to keep up with the dizzying and endless firehose of information and change. We don't feel able or willing to take on the costs of saying no to more and yes to less.

All of this adds up to what could be an overwhelm of uncertainty, which is navigatable with new questions.

Old questions do not have the power to help us navigate the uncertainties of overwhelm. Creating a new relationship with overwhelm is not a matter of better managing time or information. It's a matter of forming new questions that are more realistic.

Old questions feed the overwhelm. How do I do have as much as others seem to? How can I have it all? How can I medicate the sense of inadequacy that comes with falling short? What am I doing wrong? How can I deliver on any yes I feel obligated to deliver? What do I do with the guilt of saying no or the resentment of saying yes? How can I find less costly ways to medicate my guilt or resentment?

I've known people who rarely if ever showed up overwhelmed. I think these old questions occurred them because they live in our collective consciousness.

They simply gave attention to a whole different set of questions.

What would it mean to do things well in contrast to doing everything imaginable? Why would it take a dozen people to achieve all the things I wish I as one person could do? What do I have passion to learn that I could focus on instead of trying to keep up on everything?

What good can I contribute to my world without staying up to date on everything possible to know? What do I actually need to know in order to live a life of joy and meaning?

The tension of overwhelm is the tension of uncertainty. New questions help us live with it less.

Cultivating an inquisitive mindset

New questions visit the inquisitive mind. The inquisitive mind is a mind of wonder. We thrive on what-if questions framing new possibilities. We simply frame any wish as a what-if question.

We can wonder anywhere, anytime. Wonder sparks new questions. Anything that puzzles or perplexes us can be an object of wonder. We make our own liberation possible when we spark new questions with any kind of wonder about anything.

It was this mindset that inspired one of my most improbable, even mundane, questions. Wonder doesn't need to be restricted to the dramatic or exotic.

One late night, a friend called in a panic, stranded in a dark city parking garage. Her car wouldn't start. Launching into a litany of everything she knew about recent repairs and the trustworthiness of her mechanics, as if what she knew mattered, her only questions were old, speculative questions about causes and consequences.

My questions were about any other than hers. What's in your back seat? She reports with a fair degree of drama that someone has their things in her back seat. Breathing a sigh of relief, I suggest she look around, to which she reports seeing another car that looks just like hers.

Her lesson was about how our unknowns are more important than our knowns when we're navigating new uncertainties.

Her belief that her surface questions could be useful was all that was required to keep her from exploring more, better, different questions. I simply had no disabling fear, no belief in the questions at hand and new questions emerged, leading to new more rewarding possibilities.

The most important times to change our questions is when we believe old questions deserve our attention, instead of exploring any other questions. This is an inquisitive mindset.

For a better way, find a better why

Why do we wish for new questions? What is it about new questions that calls us? Is it that we sense new questions have a power, a magic that old questions do not? Is it that we know that we can better navigate life's constant of uncertainty with new questions than old questions?

Knowing why we want new questions unfolds how we can discover them. A clear why is enough to move forward. The answer to how is why.

As we consider any aspect of our life and world we want better, having better questions begins with understanding why we want them in the first place. Every why matters. Every why unlocks the key to new options, new possibilities.

Our why gives us the courage to explore, to listen, to consider. It gives us the clarity to live with humility, to know that what we don't know is infinitely more useful than what we know. This doesn't make knowing less important. It reveals the magic of not knowing.

We become friends with uncertainty. We cease worrying about how our life and world are and begin wondering how they could be. We become free, at last, to dream.

More beautiful questions

One of my mentors once reflected that we can only create beauty from what we understand. The more we understand ourselves, each other and our world, the more beauty we can create from it.

Beauty is peace, the opposite of fear. We fear what we don't understand. Fear of any kind, toward anything or anyone brings out the worst in us, and at least becomes a barrier to our growth. When we live without fear, we live with a sense of beauty about our lives and our world.

Peace is understanding. We are being called now as never before to create new levels of understanding. Only with deeper understanding can we live together on this planet in peace.

To create any new forms of beauty in our world together, we need to create more beautiful questions together. More beautiful questions have always been about possibilities more than problems, strengths more than weaknesses, flourishing more than survival, we more than I.

What would be new questions here? This is the quintessential inspiration for more beautiful questions in any context, in our daily routines and adventures, at work and in our communities and in the global conversations we have together.

Whether we are judged as brilliant or blundering, we always do the best we can based on our questions at the time. The only way we do better is by living from different, more beautiful questions.

This is the way of questions.

Jack Ricchiuto

For over 35 years, Jack has been helping teams, leaders, organizations and communities discover new ways to realize their potential together.

In dozens of industries globally, Jack has innovated workshops with executives and civic leaders, engineers and scientists, teachers and entrepreneurs, investors and economists, doctors and nurses, lawyers and accountants, designers and storytellers, native elders and fishermen, film makers and community builders.

As 21-time author his books focus on the psychology of flourishing, mindfulness and collaboration and include books of poetry, storytelling, photography and cooking: *Collaborative Creativity, Accidental Conversations, Project Zen, Appreciative Leadership, Mountain Paths, Conscious Becoming, Instructions from the Cook, The Stories that Connect Us, The Enchantment of Casual Origins, The Joy of Thriving,*

Ordinary Eyes, The Agile Canvas Field Guide, Abundant Possibilities, The Power Of Circles, Making Sense Of Time, Beyond Recipes, Focus, Smarter Together, Growing Ideas, The Art Of Conversations and *The Way Of Questions.*

With a graduate degree focused in positive psychology from Goddard College, Jack has taught at the Harvard Kennedy School, UC Berkeley, Vanderbilt and Kent State University. As a writer, he continues to sustain the oldest daily blog in Northern Ohio since 2002 and mentors emerging writers and entrepreneurs in their craft.

For more visit JackRicchiuto.com